LITTLE KIDS
FIRST
BIG
BOOK OF
HOW

LITTLE KIDS
FIRST
BIG
BOOK OF
HOW

Jill Esbaum

NATIONAL GEOGRAPHIC KiDS

WASHINGTON, D.C.

CONTENTS

How do microwave ovens **COOK FOOD?**

How does my house stay **WARM** in winter and **COOL** in summer?

6

AROUND THE HOME

Microwave

How does a vacuum cleaner **SWALLOW UP DIRT?**

HOW DOES MY HOUSE STAY WARM IN WINTER AND COOL IN SUMMER?

Before furnaces, people often had **FIREPLACES** to heat a room or two. At bedtime, they sometimes tucked **FIRE-HEATED BRICKS** under the covers of their cold beds to warm their feet.

A furnace keeps your home warm when it's cold outside. It heats the air inside the house. Then a fan blows that warm air through **ductwork** to every corner of your home.

Air conditioners keep your home cool in summer. They pull in outdoor air and chill it before a fan blows it through your home.

How warm or cool do you want your house to be? You select that temperature on an instrument called a **thermostat.** The thermostat senses your home's air temperature. If it's too cool, the thermostat signals the furnace to start. If it's too warm, the thermostat starts the air conditioner.

What's inside the walls helps keep your home cozy, too. Usually, there's a thick padding or foamlike material called **insulation** in the walls. Insulation blocks outside air from coming inside.

9

HOW DOES ELECTRICITY GET TO MY HOME?

Flip a switch, and a light goes on. Plug in a cord, and electricity makes things like fans, hair dryers, and toasters work. But that electricity travels a long way to get to your home.

FACTS

What do we use to make **ELECTRICITY?**

Wind, water, sun, and even **ANIMAL POOP.**

A kind of fish called an **ELECTRIC EEL** makes electricity within its body.

Lightning is electricity in the air. A bolt of **LIGHTNING** can be as hot as 54,000°F (30,000°C).

A bird can perch on a **POWER LINE** without being hurt as long as it does not touch a second line at the same time.

10

Most electricity is made in places called **power plants.** Power plants send large amounts of electricity through thick, tough wires called high-voltage lines. The electricity arrives at smaller buildings called substations. There, the electricity is divided into smaller amounts and sent on through smaller lines to homes and businesses.

At your home, electricity goes into the service panel. From there, it travels through the **wires** hidden inside your walls, ceilings, and floors to outlets and switches.

How **FAST** does **ELECTRICITY** travel? Pretend there's a lightbulb on the moon, and the switch to turn it on is in your bedroom. When you flip the switch, **IT TAKES JUST OVER ONE SECOND** for the electricity to travel to the moon and light the bulb.

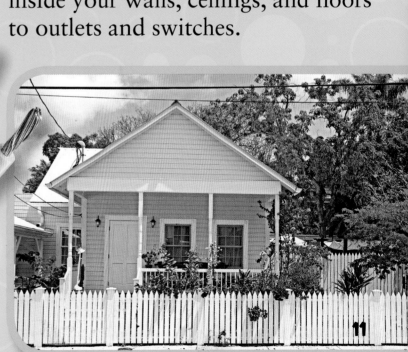

11

HOW ARE TREES MADE INTO WOODEN FLOORS?

First, trees are cut into logs. Workers check to make sure there aren't very many knots. Knotted spots are weak and might crack easily.

12

Saws cut the logs into thick boards called planks. A machine sands the planks to smooth away jagged saw marks. Another machine cuts **tongue-and-groove** edges into the planks. When laid side by side to make a floor, each plank's tongue fits tightly into another plank's groove.

People experiment with new flooring materials, such as **BAMBOO, CONCRETE, CORK, RUBBER, GLASS,** and even **LEATHER,** pennies, or **BOTTLE CAPS!**

Many farms grow trees especially for flooring and cabinetmaking. Some of the most popular trees for these uses are oak, ash, walnut, maple, hickory, pine, beech, and cherry.

13

HOW DOES A HAIR DRYER MAKE HEAT?

A hair dryer has a bare, coiled wire called a **heating element** inside it. When you switch on the dryer, electricity heats the wire until it is red-hot. A small fan pulls air into one end of the dryer. As the air travels across the heating element, it gets hot. That hot air blows out through the dryer's **nozzle.**

HAIR DRYERS are used for more than drying hair. Sometimes people use them to thaw **FROZEN DOOR LOCKS**, dry **PAINT** quickly, soften **ICE CREAM**, and even to dry a **DOG'S WET FUR**.

It takes only about half a second to heat the cool air sucked into a hair dryer and blow it out the other end. If the air stayed inside the dryer any longer, it would get too hot and burn your hair.

A **COILED WIRE** is one that is wound around and around **TIGHTLY**, like a spring.

15

HOW DOES A DOORBELL WORK?

Ding-dong! **Someone's at the door!**

Some doorbells are electric. Pushing a button sends a zap of electricity to a special magnet called an **electromagnet.** It is turned on and off instantly by electricity. When the electromagnet zaps on, it causes a **little hammer** to hit a bell, buzzer, or chime bars.

SOME PEOPLE are deaf, which means they can't hear. They can use **DOORBELLS** that **FLASH LIGHTS** instead of making noise.

Other doorbells are called clappers. When you push a button, you cause two small pieces of metal to touch by clapping together. Electricity flows from one piece of metal to the other. That makes a little hammer strike a bell. *Ding!* When your finger leaves the button, a small spring pushes the button back out again.

There are **DOORBELLS** that play music, **BOOM** like thunder, or make **ANIMAL SOUNDS.**

17

HOW DO MICROWAVE OVENS COOK FOOD?

Everything everywhere is made up of tiny parts called molecules. Don't bother looking for them. Molecules are too tiny to see without a powerful microscope.

When you put food into a microwave oven and push START, invisible waves of heat called microwaves hit the **water molecules** inside the food. The heat makes the molecules vibrate, or move back and forth quickly.

All that vibrating makes the heat that cooks your food. The faster the molecules vibrate, the hotter the food gets. As the microwaves bounce around inside the oven, they hit the food from all sides.

POPCORN is one of the most common foods cooked in **MICROWAVE OVENS,** which usually have a special "popcorn" **CONTROL BUTTON.**

19

HOW DO REFRIGERATORS STAY COLD?

Some foods need to be kept cold to stay safe to eat. The best place for that is inside a cold refrigerator.

Have you ever heard your refrigerator's motor running? It works hard to run an air-cooling machine called a compressor.

A **thermostat** inside the refrigerator senses temperature—how cold or hot it is inside the refrigerator. If the air gets too warm, the thermostat sends a signal to the motor, which turns on the compressor.

20

OPEN DOOR INVESTIGATION

How many times each day do you think you open your refrigerator? Keep a paper and pencil on a kitchen counter. Have everybody in your family make a mark each time they open the refrigerator door. Is the number of times your family opens the refrigerator higher or lower than your guess?

5

27

22

10

18

10

20

HOW DOES A VACUUM CLEANER SWALLOW UP DIRT?

When you drink juice through a straw into your mouth, you are using suction. A vacuum cleaner uses suction, too. But it sucks up air.

BEFORE vacuum cleaners were invented, people **HUNG THEIR RUGS OUTDOORS** and used a tool made of **BENT WOOD** or **WIRE** to beat the dirt out of them.

A vacuum cleaner's motor runs a powerful **fan.** As the fan spins, its blades move air through the machine.

Dirt and dust get sucked up with the air and pushed through the vacuum. The dirt and dust are collected in a container inside the vacuum as the air moves out.

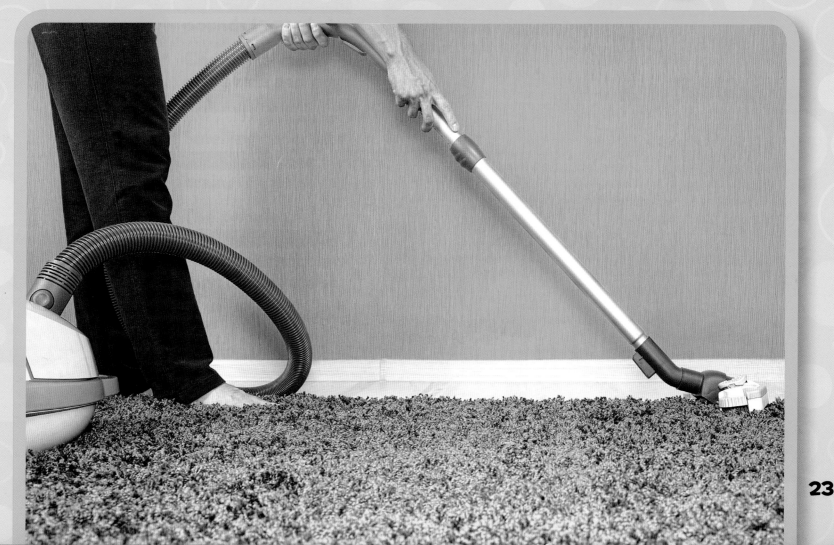

HOW DOES WATER COME OUT OF THE FAUCET?

If you live in a town or city, your water comes from deep underground or from a river or lake. The water goes to a place called a water treatment facility, where it is tested and treated to be sure it is clean and safe to drink.

That clean water flows through underground pipes—under streets, sidewalks, and yards—until it reaches the pipes connected to your home's faucets.

water treatment facility

FACTS

Most of the Earth is covered **WITH WATER.**

About 750,000 gallons (3,000,000 L) of water go over **NIAGARA FALLS** every second.

Most of the water Americans use each day is for flushing **TOILETS.**

One gallon (4L) of water weighs a little over eight pounds (4 kg). That's about what a **HOUSE CAT** weighs.

A stopper inside each faucet keeps water from gushing out until you turn the faucet on. Not all faucets are alike. Some need a twist to open the stopper. Some need a nudge. Some need only a wave of your hand.

If you live far from a city, your water probably comes from a well near your home. A well is a deep hole that was drilled with special machines to reach water that flows underground. An electric pump inside the well pulls water up into a storage tank and then pushes it through pipes into your home.

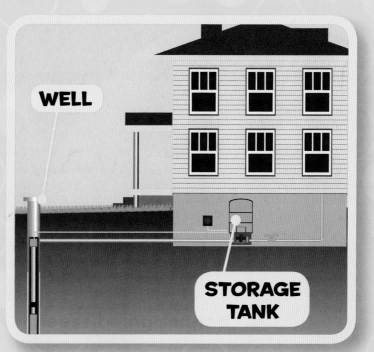

WELL

STORAGE TANK

LET'S PLAY A GAME!

Look at the pictures of a house below. Can you find the ten things in the picture on the right that are different from the picture on the left?

1. Apples removed from tree in kitchen window; 2. Purple car in garage changed to green; 3. Pillows and blankets missing from beds; 4. Barbell removed from table at bottom of stairs; 5. Baby bottles moved to chair in baby's room; 6. Handles missing from laundry room cabinets; 7. Red lamp removed from bedroom dresser; 8. Green kitchen light changed to red; 9. Bathroom shade pulled down; 10. Picture removed from living room.

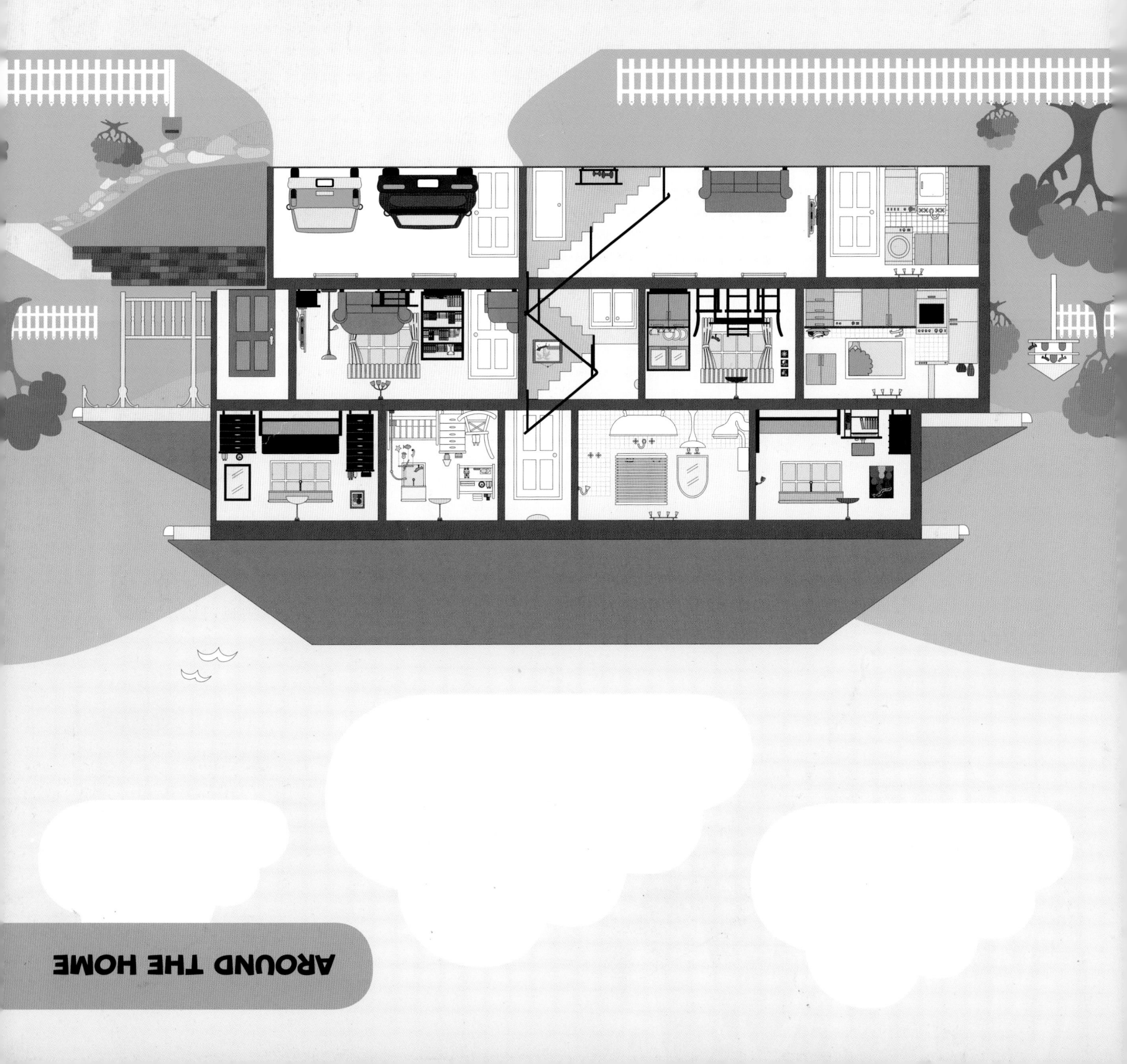

AROUND THE HOME

How are
**CARS
PAINTED?**

How do
bicycle gears
**CHANGE
SPEEDS?**

28

2

COMING AND GOING

How fast are the world's FASTEST TRAINS?

Have you ridden a bike **WITH GEARS?**

HOW DO BICYCLE GEARS CHANGE SPEEDS?

Many bikes have one speed: as fast as a rider pedals! Others have three speeds, five speeds, or as many as twenty-seven!

Bikes with more than one speed have two or three chainrings on their front wheels and seven to eleven cogs on the back wheel. **Chainrings and cogs** are made of metal and have teeth that hold a bike's chain in place.

Each year, about **100 MILLION** new bicycles roll into the world.

To shift from one gear to another, a rider slides the **shifter** on the handlebars. That moves the chain from one chainring or cog to another of a different size. That makes pedaling easier or harder.

Pretend you are riding along a flat path on a three-speed bike in second gear. Then you come to a hill. Halfway up, you are having a hard time pedaling. What should you do? Shift down into first gear. Pedaling is suddenly much easier!

HOW ARE CARS PAINTED?

New cars are painted in the factory where they are made. Many parts are painted before the cars are put together. If a car's owner wants it repainted for some reason—such as scratches or chips—the car goes to a shop that fixes cars one at a time. No matter what color a car is, its owner wants the paint to look shiny and smooth.

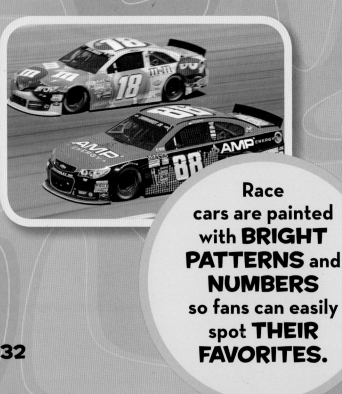

Race cars are painted with **BRIGHT PATTERNS** and **NUMBERS** so fans can easily spot **THEIR FAVORITES.**

Workers paint cars with spraying machines in large, extremely clean rooms. If dirt or dust gets on the cars, it will make the paint bumpy. People who work in these rooms have to be clean, too. They even wear special suits.

Each paint job ends with a final layer of see-through paint called clear coat. After that dries, cars are inspected very closely with a special camera. No specks allowed!

COLORS OF THE ROAD INVESTIGATION

You can do this experiment the next time you take a car ride. You'll need paper and a pencil.

Across the top of a page, write common car colors: white, silver, red, yellow, black, and blue. For five minutes (or set a longer time limit if you wish), watch the cars driving by and make small check marks under the colors of the cars you see. At the end of the five minutes, stop.

Which color did you see most often? Do any of your colors have no checks under them?

white	silver	red	yellow	black	blue
✓	✓	✓		✓	✓
✓	✓	✓		✓	
✓	✓			✓	
		✓		✓	
		✓			
		✓			

HOW ARE ROADS MADE?

Machines like bulldozers, graders, and dump trucks help workers build roads. First, workers move dirt around. They shape and flatten the roadbed, which is where cars will drive.

bulldozer

Next, they spread layers of **gravel,** a mixture of small stones, on top of the roadbed. Heavy machines roll over the gravel, pressing it into a hard, flat surface.

grader

roller

VERY HOT temperatures make concrete **EXPAND,** or get bigger. **VERY COLD** temperatures make concrete **CONTRACT,** or get smaller. Expanding and contracting **MAKES CRACKS IN HIGHWAYS.** To keep this from happening, workers cut lines called **JOINTS** into new concrete that allow it to expand and contract without cracking.

A hot, oily mixture of sand and crushed rock called **asphalt** is used on some roads. Others are covered with wet concrete. Both asphalt and concrete dry hard and tough.

When the road is dry, machines paint lines along the road's sides and down the middle. Sometimes special tiny beads are mixed into the paint. The beads reflect light when headlights shine on them. This helps drivers see the lines at night or in the rain.

TUNNELS are sometimes built **UNDER HIGHWAYS** so wild animals like deer, moose, bobcats, and bears can **SAFELY CROSS** to the other side.

35

beam bridge

HOW ARE BRIDGES BUILT ACROSS WATER?

There are three basic types of bridges: beam, arch, and suspension. Each is built in a different way.

suspension bridge

arch bridge

For beam bridges over wide bodies of water, builders begin by standing huge steel or concrete support pillars into the bottom of the river, lake, or bay. Then they lay strong beams across the pillars. Finally, a road is built on top.

To build an arch bridge, builders start from each side and build toward the middle. Strong steel cables hold up each side until the bridge halves come together.

Workers building a suspension bridge also start from each side and meet in the middle. Giant steel cables fastened tightly at each end of the bridge help hold it up.

The world's **LONGEST ROAD** bridge is in Thailand. The **BANG NA EXPRESSWAY BRIDGE** is 34 miles (55 km) long. It takes about **20 MINUTES** to drive across it.

HOW DO CRANES GET TO THE TOP OF HIGH BUILDINGS?

To **GET INTO THEIR CRANES,** operators have to climb up **VERY TALL** ladders.

Cranes get to the top of buildings in three different ways.

The first way a crane can get to the top of a building is called external climbing. The crane sits outside the bottom of a new building. It is attached to the building by steel bars called struts. As the building gets taller, new struts are added to lift the crane.

A crane can also get to the top of a building by internal climbing. A crane is placed in the middle of a building. Workers build around the crane. When the crane can no longer reach the work, a special machine under the crane pushes it up to a higher floor. Workers slide steel beams under the crane, and when it needs to move higher again, the machine pushes up from those beams. Up and up and up it goes!

Sometimes a crane is taken apart, and a heavy-lift helicopter flies the pieces to the top of a building. Workers fit the pieces together and get to work.

39

HOW ARE TIRES MADE?

Tires are made of rubber and are molded, sort of like waffles.

First, sheets of rubber, recycled tires, and certain liquids are mixed together in giant containers. All that mixing creates heat that softens the rubber. Machinery squishes the rubber and rolls it into new sheets. The rubber sheets are washed in soapy water, and then they are hung to dry.

The rubber is made tougher by adding steel, ropelike cords, and nylon—a strong, stretchy fabric. The rubber is **shaped into a loop** called a band. The band fits onto what looks like a big drum. After a few more steps, the tire is removed from the machine to cool.

The world's **LARGEST** tire, built for fun, stands near the Detroit, **MICHIGAN**, U.S.A., airport. It was once used as a **FERRIS WHEEL!**

The world's **BIGGEST** tires used on vehicles are taller than **ELEPHANTS.** Just one of these tires weighs as much as two pickup trucks.

41

HOW FAST ARE THE WORLD'S FASTEST TRAINS?

? Have **YOU** ever tried to count train cars as they **WHOOSHED** past?

The fastest train in the world, called the **Shanghai Maglev,** operates in China. This train can travel as fast as 268 miles an hour (430 km/h). That's more than four times faster than your parents drive on the highway.

The speediest train in North America is Amtrak's **Acela Express.** It takes passengers between Boston, Massachusetts, and Washington, D.C. The Acela is able to travel as fast as 150 miles an hour (241 km/h).

The **LONGEST TRAIN** in the world carried **IRON ORE**—rocks that contain iron—in Australia. It took **8 ENGINES TO PULL** the **682 CARS.**

HOW DO SUBMARINES STAY UNDERWATER?

ballast tank controls

Powerful engines help submarines stay underwater. But ballast tanks are important, too. Ballast tanks are large compartments, sort of like giant metal pockets, inside a submarine. They hold air or water. Workers control how much air and water go into and out of the tanks.

U.S. Navy submarines can **DIVE 800 FEET** (244 m) deep.

BERTHS, which is what beds in submarines are called, are stacked three high.

When they aren't working, sailors **PLAY CARDS** and games or watch movies.

To go underwater, workers let air out of the ballast tanks, allowing seawater to rush in. Water is heavier than the air it replaced, so the sub becomes heavier and is able to stay underwater.

When the sub needs to come to the surface, crew members flip a switch that causes air to be blown into its ballast tanks. The air forces the seawater out. Air-filled tanks are light. That helps the sub rise to the surface and stay there.

COMING AND GOING

When a **SUBMARINE** is deep underwater, its crew **CANNOT SEE** outside. There are no windows. **COMPUTERS** tell the crew where they are.

Modern submarines **DISTILL** seawater to remove the salt while they're out to sea. With such a **PRECIOUS WATER SUPPLY,** crew members never leave water running while **BRUSHING THEIR TEETH,** washing their hands, or even showering.

HOW ARE ROCKETS LAUNCHED INTO SPACE?

A rocket is attached to huge tanks of fuel. When the fuel burns, it pushes hot gas out of the back of the rocket. This is called **thrust.** A rocket's thrust is powerful! It lifts the heavy rocket off the launchpad and pushes it up into the sky. When the rocket is high enough to escape Earth's gravity, it has reached space.

GRAVITY is the invisible force that **PULLS** things toward **EARTH.**

Communications **SATELLITES SEND SIGNALS** that make our cell phones, televisions, and radios **WORK.**

Rockets are used for many things. Sometimes rockets carry people into space. Rockets are also used to place **communications satellites** high above Earth. They send exploration tools into space, too. Those tools collect information about space and other planets, and send it back to scientists on Earth.

International Space Station

Rockets are also used to send supplies like food, fuel, equipment for experiments, and other supplies to the International Space Station (ISS). The ISS is a science lab in space. Since 2000, six astronauts at a time have lived and worked on the ISS as it circles the Earth. Astronauts usually stay about six months before riding back to Earth in a Russian space vehicle called the **Soyuz.**

47

LET'S PLAY A GAME!

Look at all these things you've read about in this chapter. Can you put their names in alphabetical order?

Paint

Grader

Road

Bridge

A B C D E F G H I J K L M

48

Tire

Submarine

Express train

Crane

N O P Q R S T U V W X Y Z

How do my
EYES SEE?

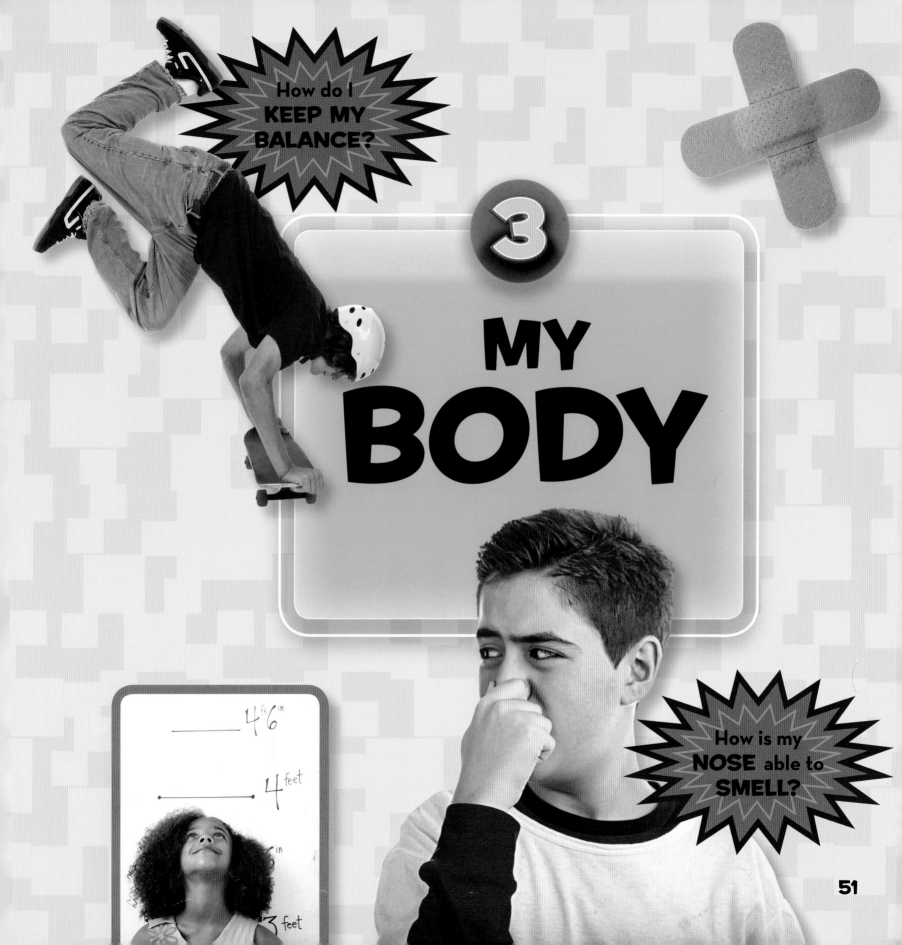

How do I
**KEEP MY
BALANCE?**

3

MY
BODY

How is my
NOSE able to
SMELL?

HOW DO I CATCH A COLD?

Colds are caused by germs called viruses.
If we could see a yucky cold virus on a **doorknob,** we wouldn't touch it. But viruses are too small to see without a powerful microscope.

Pretend your friend has a cold. You shake hands, stand too close, or simply borrow a pencil just as your friend sneezes. *Achoo!* That can be all it takes for a few of your friend's cold germs to get on your fingers. Then you touch your nose or mouth, and those cold germs are in you.

The **cold germs** attach themselves to the soft places in your nose or throat. Your body sends white blood cells—its germ fighters—to attack the germs. That might work. If not, your nose and throat get red. Your nose fights the germs by making a thick bacteria attacker called mucus. In a few days, the cold is usually gone.

It is **NORMAL** for kids to have about **SEVEN COLDS** every year.

You are **MORE LIKELY** to catch a cold when you are **TIRED.** So get plenty of sleep!

53

HOW DO I HEAL?

BROKEN BONES

A bone break is called a fracture (FRAK-chur). **X-rays** show a doctor exactly where the fracture is and whether it's a small, thin crack or a bone snapped into two pieces.

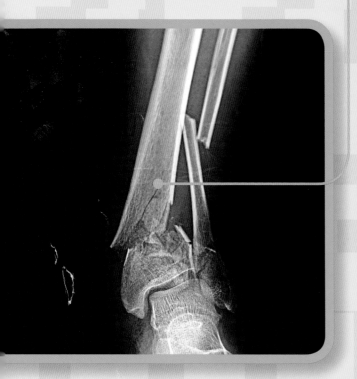

First, a doctor carefully sets the bone back into its normal position. Usually, the doctor uses a **cast**—a special hard bandage—to hold the reset bone in place.

Then your bones go to work. For the next month or two they make new cells, which are your body's building blocks, and tiny blood vessels to fill in that held-together spot with strong, new bone.

CUTS AND SCRAPES

Your body has platelets (PLATE-lutz) that work to stop bleeding. Whenever your skin gets hurt, platelets rush to the cut and stick together like glue. They block the damaged area so no more blood leaks out.

When the platelets dry, they form a hard scab that protects the area. Underneath, skin cells are working hard. When they have finished making a new layer of skin, the scab falls off.

? Have **YOU** ever **BROKEN** a **BONE?**

A **KID'S BROKEN BONE** heals faster than an **ADULT'S.**

HOW DO I GROW?

You can't feel it, but there's a **chemical constantly** flowing through your body called human growth hormone. This chemical works day and night (but mostly at night!) to help you grow.

Some kids **GROW FASTER** than others. But the best way to grow is to get **EIGHT TO TEN HOURS OF SLEEP** every night, exercise, and eat healthy foods.

Kids grow **FASTER** in **SPRING AND SUMMER** than any other time of **YEAR.**

As your bones grow longer, you grow taller. Slowly, every part of your body gains weight and strength. You cannot feel yourself growing, but you notice it when your pant legs get too short or your toes suddenly jam up against the inside of your shoes!

57

HOW DO MY EYES SEE?

When you look at **anything,** light rays bounce off of the object and into your eyes. The light rays go through the small black hole in the middle of each eye called the pupil.

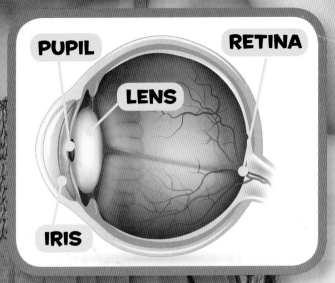

PUPIL   RETINA

LENS

IRIS

The light rays travel through a thin lens to the back of each eye. That's where light arrives at the retina, which turns those light rays into signals that your brain can understand.

Your iris, the colored part around your pupil, is actually a muscle. Its job is to control how much light gets into the eye. When you are in a bright place, the iris shrinks the pupil to let in less light. When you are in a darker place, the pupil opens to let in more light to help you see better.

You blink more than **10,000 TIMES A DAY.** Blinking helps keep your eyes **CLEAN** and **MOIST.**

SHRINKING PUPILS INVESTIGATION

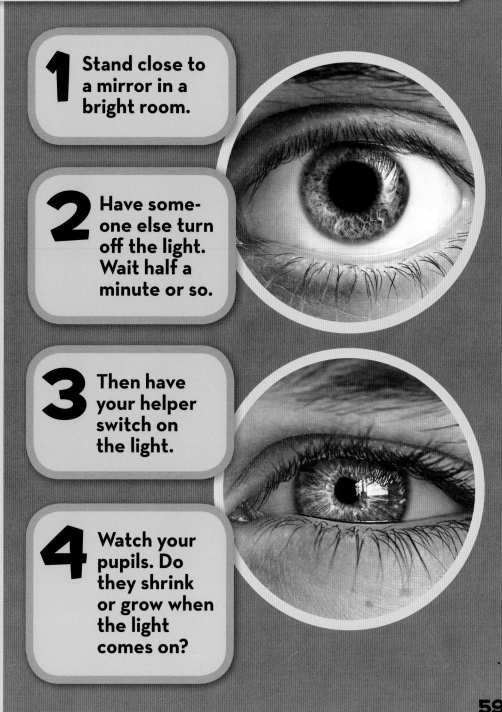

1 Stand close to a mirror in a bright room.

2 Have someone else turn off the light. Wait half a minute or so.

3 Then have your helper switch on the light.

4 Watch your pupils. Do they shrink or grow when the light comes on?

HOW IS MY NOSE ABLE TO SMELL?

? What is the **STINKIEST** thing you've ever **SMELLED?**

Smelling starts with the two holes at the bottom of your nose called nostrils. That's where air goes in. It moves into a big open space called your **nasal cavity.** The nasal cavity is behind your nose and above the hard roof of your mouth.

The olfactory epithelium (ol-FAK-tor-ee eh-puh-THEE-lee-um) is hard at work inside your nasal cavity. Wow, that's hard to say! Let's call it your smelling factory.

Inside that smelling factory, special receptors notice and recognize smells. The receptors are too small to see. How small? Your nose might have ten million of them!

When those receptors notice a smell, they send signals to your brain. Yech, my shoes stink! or Ooh, chocolate chip cookies! or That's a rose!

HUMAN BRAINS can recognize thousands of DIFFERENT SMELLS.

HOW DOES MY TONGUE TASTE FOODS?

Look at your tongue in a mirror. See those little bumps? They're called papillae (puh-PILL-ee), and most of them contain taste buds with teeny, tiny hairs. When something touches the hairs, they send a message to your brain that tells it whether the taste is sweet, salty, bitter, sour, or just plain yucky.

You have about **10,000 TASTE BUDS** on your tongue. **AND GUESS WHAT?** They wear out! But new ones replace them about every **TEN DAYS.**

THE NOSE KNOWS INVESTIGATION

Your nose plays a part in tasting, too. Take a bite of food, and think about how it tastes. Now, hold your nose and take another bite. Notice anything different?

FACTS

Your tongue contains **EIGHT MUSCLES.**

Human tongues are about **FOUR INCHES (10 cm)** long.

A BLUE WHALE'S tongue weighs as much as an elephant.

Your tongue and **YOUR THROAT** have taste buds.

Food and drink companies **HIRE PEOPLE just** to taste and judge new products.

Three little fluid-filled tubes sit deep inside each of your ears. They are lined with tiny hairs. Every time you move around, the fluid in the tubes sloshes around too, moving the hairs. Those hairs send signals to your brain that tell your body how to move to keep its balance.

If you spin in circles and then stop, you feel dizzy. That's because the liquid inside your ear tubes is still sloshing. The little hairs are still telling your brain that your body is spinning, so it gets confused. After a while, the sloshing stops. The hairs stop moving, and you stop feeling dizzy.

HOW DO I KEEP MY BALANCE?

HOW DO I FALL ASLEEP?

It's late at night, and your eyelids feel heavy. You are having a hard time keeping your head up. Your sight and hearing seem to get fuzzy. Your brain is trying to tell you that it is ready for sleep.

You fall asleep in stages—one step at a time.

Stage 1: Your eyes have just closed. You can wake up easily.

Stage 2: Your muscles relax. Your breathing is slow and even. So is your heartbeat.

Stage 3: You are hard to wake up. You might talk or kick. Some people even sleepwalk, which is when they get up and walk around.

Stage 4: You're in a very deep sleep. If someone wakes you now, you feel groggy and confused.

You go into and out of stages 2, 3, and 4 throughout the night. About five times each night, you will also be in a REM stage of sleep. REM stands for "rapid eye movement." It is during REM sleep that you dream.

Some people see **NO COLOR** in their dreams. Everything is **BLACK AND WHITE** or shades of **GRAY**.

LET'S PLAY A GAME!

Use the pictures to help you read this story about how a boy named Mason and his sister Sophia use their five senses.

___ went along to his baby sister ___'s, checkup.

In the ___'s waiting room, ___ scanned

the room with his ___. He saw a boy with a ___.

Nearby, a lady held a .

66

's mom gave him a bag of 🍎 slices.

He smelled them with his 👃 before sharing them with

👧 . The 🍎 tasted sweet on his 👅 .

After their snack, 👦 helped 👧 practice walking.

 held his sister's tiny ✋ as she balanced on

wobbly 👖 . Her giggles made everybody  .

67

How do camels **STAY COOL** in the desert?

How do brown bears **STAY ASLEEP** during hibernation?

THE
ANIMAL
KINGDOM

4

How do
chameleons
**CHANGE
COLOR?**

OW DO CHAMELEONS CHANGE COLOR?

Chameleons change their skin color to warm or cool their bodies or to communicate with other chameleons. Scientists say that chameleons can change color on purpose.

The upper layers of a chameleon's skin have cells filled with very tiny bits of pigment, or color. The deepest layer has black or brown pigment. The middle layer has blue pigment. The top layer has yellow and red pigments.

A chameleon's brain sends signals to its color cells, depending on whether the animal is too cold or too warm, or what it needs to communicate to another animal. These signals make the color cells open wider or shrink. That widening or shrinking allows different cells to reflect light, changing the chameleon's skin color.

It takes about **20 SECONDS** for a chameleon's skin to change color.

Not all beavers build their homes **INSIDE DAMS.** If the animals live near a pond or lake, or along a river, they simply **BURROW INTO A MUDDY BANK** and create a home inside. This is called a **BANK DEN.**

FACTS

Beaver babies are **CALLED KITS.**

BEAVER TEETH never stop growing.

Beavers are rodents, like **RATS, MICE, AND SQUIRRELS.**

While swimming, a beaver's strong, **FLAT TAIL** helps it steer.

One beaver dam in Canada is so big it **CAN BE SEEN FROM SPACE.**

HOW DOES A BEAVER BUILD A DAM?

Beaver families work together to build their dams. First, they gnaw down young trees with their two sharp front teeth. Then they drag these long tree poles to the narrowest spot in a creek or stream. They stack the poles, tucking the ends of each one over and under others. Beavers plug cracks with sticks and gravel and mud.

Sometimes beavers make a home, called a **lodge,** inside a dam. They build separate rooms for eating and nesting, and these rooms stay dry. Lodges include an underwater entrance or two, plus a hole that lets in fresh air.

71

HOW DO JELLYFISH STING?

Just one touch of a jellyfish's long, soft tentacles and—ouch! Faster than you can blink, you have been stung.

The **tentacles** hanging from a jellyfish's body contain tiny tube-like cells filled with venom—a poisonous liquid. When something touches a tentacle, the cells shoot their venom. They shoot so hard they turn themselves inside out, like when you take off a wet glove.

STINGING helps a jellyfish defend itself from **DANGER** or **CAPTURE FISH** or other prey.

HOW DO OCTOPUSES SQUIRT INK?

When an octopus is startled or afraid, it squirts dark ink made inside its body. The ink shoots from a sac, along with water from a body opening called a **siphon** (SIE-fen), and helps hide the octopus so it can escape. The siphon is the same opening from which an octopus shoots out water to help it swim. It is also where an octopus releases its body's waste materials.

Octopus ink is made up of a dark brown or black coloring called melanin. Melanin is the same thing that colors a human's skin and dark hair. It has something in it that hurts the eyes of a predator. It also makes it hard for the other animal to smell.

FACTS

Octopuses are **MEAT-EATERS.**

The smallest octopus, the **WOLFI,** could sit on a penny.

Octopuses have **NO BONES.**

Octopuses have **THREE HEARTS.**

The suction cups on an octopus's arms **CAN TASTE** what they're touching.

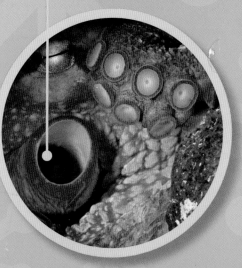

73

HOW DO BROWN BEARS STAY ASLEEP DURING HIBERNATION?

In the fall, brown bears eat as much as **possible** to build up their fat. Then they dig a den or find a hollow place under a tree or in a pile of rocks to curl up and sleep. While they hibernate, their bodies use all that extra fat to stay alive.

Brown bears **HIBERNATE** for up to **EIGHT MONTHS** a year.

Bears often wake up during hibernation. They move around inside their dens. They might even take a walk outside. But their favorite foods—nuts and berries—are gone or covered with snow, so they return to their dens and go back to sleep. *Zzzzz.*

Females give birth during hibernation and wake up enough to care for their cubs.

SLEEP LIKE A BEAR INVESTIGATION

Bears spend the winter months hibernating. That's a lot of sleep! How long do you sleep each night?

Make a chart marked with the seven days of the week. Write down how many hours you sleep each night.

Make a happy face on the days you get up feeling wide awake and cheerful. Make a sad face when you wake up feeling sleepy and grumpy.

Does the amount of sleep you get make a difference in how you feel in the morning?

MONDAY	TUESDAY	WEDNESDAY	THURSDAY	FRIDAY	SATURDAY	SUNDAY
8	10	9	8	7	10	7

DON'T FORGET: _____

A hibernating bear **BREATHES MORE SLOWLY** while asleep, and its heartbeat drops to only **10 BEATS** a minute from its usual **45 BEATS** a minute.

HOW DO RATTLESNAKES RATTLE?

A rattlesnake **VIBRATES ITS TAIL** as many as **90 TIMES** a second and can keep it up for hours.

A rattlesnake is born with a rounded tip on its tail that looks sort of like a button. Rattlesnakes shed their skin several times a year. Every time a rattlesnake sheds its skin, a little bit of it gets stuck on that button. The skin dries into hard, thin layers like fingernails. In this way, segments, or sections, are always being added to a snake's rattle.

A rattlesnake vibrates its tail—moving it back and forth quickly—as a warning that it is ready to fight to defend itself. When the tail vibrates, those dry segments click together to make a rattling sound.

A rattlesnake's tail doesn't get longer and longer and longer. Bits are always breaking off. This does not hurt the snake, and it doesn't miss the rattles. More layers are on their way!

HOW DO CAMELS STAY COOL IN THE DESERT?

A camel's thick hair is like a heavy wool coat. This coat keeps the camel warm at night, and it helps the camel's body stay cool by protecting it from desert heat during the day.

Everything about a camel's body is designed for desert life. Its feet are wide and thickly padded, so walking on loose sand is easy. Thick eyelashes and hairy ears keep out blowing dust and sand. A camel can even close its nostrils!

Best of all, camels store fat in their humps and water in their stomach lining. If a camel has to go without food or water for a while, its body uses this stored fat and water to keep it alive.

DROMEDARY camels have **ONE HUMP** and live in parts of the Middle East and Africa. **BACTRIAN** camels have **TWO HUMPS** and live in parts of Asia.

HOW DO HUMPBACK WHALES COMMUNICATE WITH EACH OTHER?

Humpbacks communicate in many ways. Males sing beautiful songs. Every male in a group of whales, called a pod, sings the same song. At first, scientists thought the males sang their songs to attract females. But then they watched females to see how they acted when the males sang. The females didn't seem to care.

Male and female humpbacks often make *bloop-bloop-bloop* sounds while eating. They groan and moan. They squeal. They slap their tails on the water's surface. All these whale sounds must be ways of communicating with others. But nobody is sure exactly what the sounds mean.

Nobody knows exactly how the sounds are made either. Scientists are pretty sure the whales make the sounds inside their heads. But no air bubbles come out of whales making these sounds, and their mouths stay closed.

How whales make their sounds and sing their songs— and what they mean—are mysteries scientists hope to solve someday.

Humpback whales can weigh as much as **THREE SCHOOL BUSES.** That's up to 40 tons (36,287 kg)! Yet they are strong enough **TO BREACH, OR LEAP COMPLETELY UP ABOVE,** the water's surface.

HOW DO SCIENTISTS KNOW HOW TO PUT DINOSAUR SKELETONS TOGETHER?

When paleontologists find **SHARP TEETH,** they know that dinosaur was a meat-eater. **FLAT TEETH** tell them the dinosaur was a plant-eater. **CAN YOU GUESS WHY?**

Scientists who study fossils, or the preserved remains of ancient animals or plants, are called paleontologists.

Paleontologists know a lot about dinosaur bones. A bone's shape tells them whether it was part of a dinosaur's arm or foot or spine or tail. That helps them know how the bones fit together. If they can't figure it out, they look at other dinosaur skeletons to see where it might fit in.

But it is rare to find an entire dinosaur skeleton. Usually, only a few bones are found. Sometimes, bits and pieces of different dinosaurs are found jumbled together. Then paleontologists have a real puzzle to work out. Which bones belonged to which dinosaur?

Luckily, paleontologists discovered that dinosaur skeletons fit together very much like the skeletons of birds living today. Studying bird skeletons gives them clues about how unfamiliar dinosaur bones fit together.

81

LET'S PLAY A GAME!

A pattern is something that repeats. The animals make three patterns in the three rows in this game. Can you say which animal belongs in each of the three empty circles?

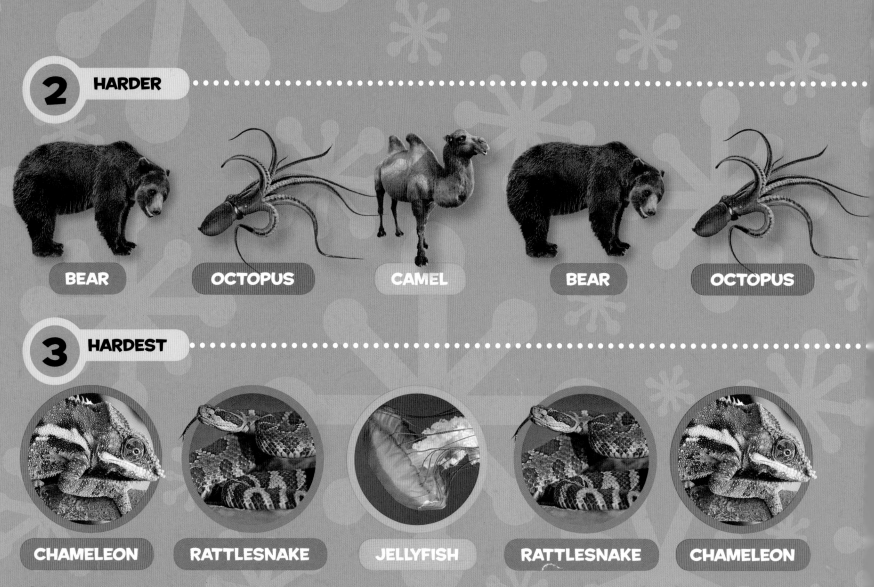

2 HARDER

BEAR | OCTOPUS | CAMEL | BEAR | OCTOPUS

3 HARDEST

CHAMELEON | RATTLESNAKE | JELLYFISH | RATTLESNAKE | CHAMELEON

1 EASY

BEAVER WHALE BEAVER WHALE ?

CAMEL BEAR OCTOPUS CAMEL ?

RATTLESNAKE JELLYFISH RATTLESNAKE CHAMELEON ?

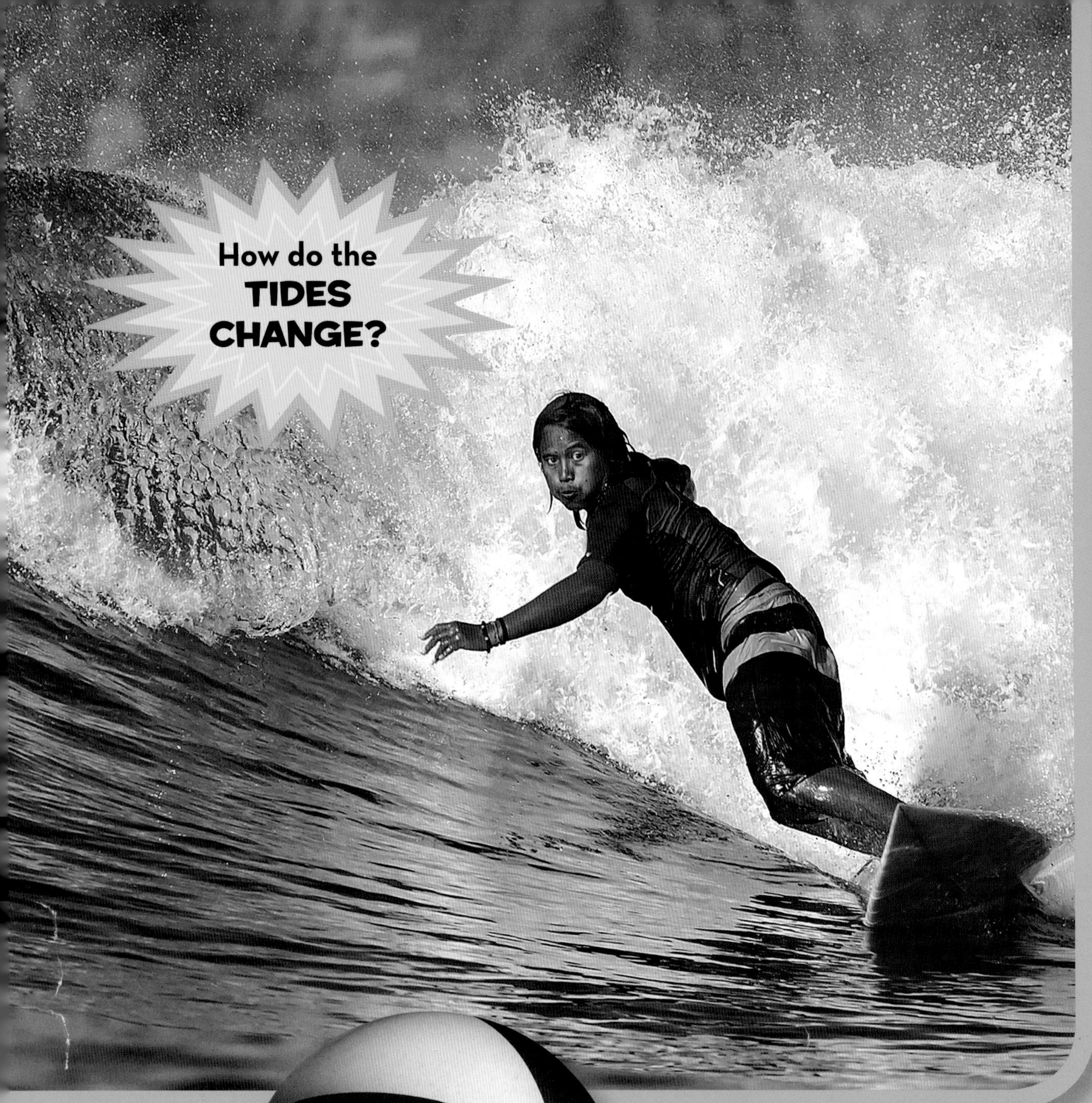

How do the **TIDES CHANGE?**

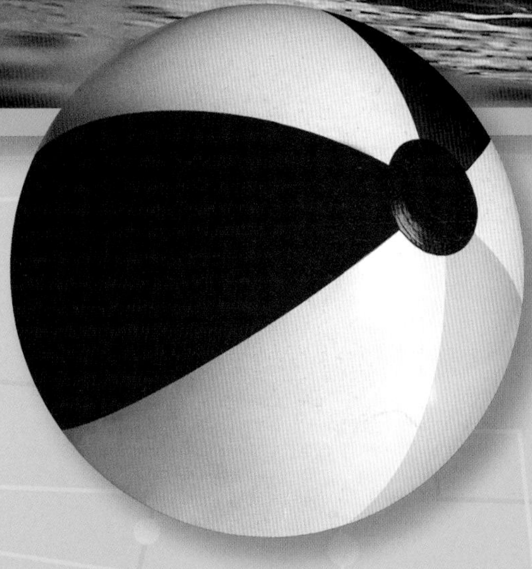

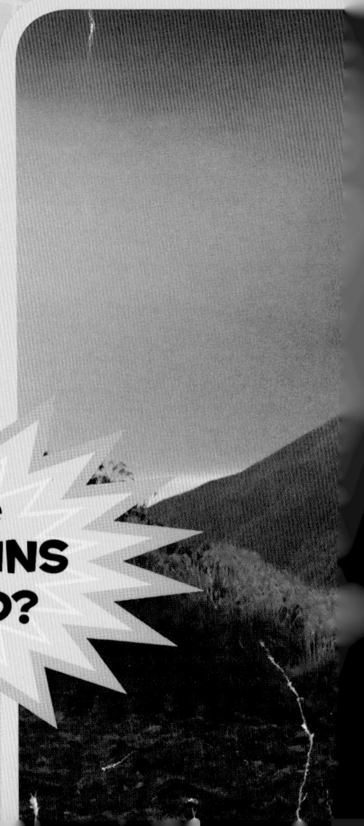

How are **MOUNTAINS FORMED?**

How do
**TORNADOES
FORM?**

5

THE GREAT OUTDOORS

HOW DOES HAIL FORM?

During **strong thunderstorms, powerful winds** sometimes swoop upward, taking raindrops with them. It's colder at the top of a storm. Raindrops freeze up there. The wind blows those icy drops up and down, up and down, through the storm. The drops keep collecting more ice. Finally, they get too heavy, and they fall to Earth. That is **hail.**

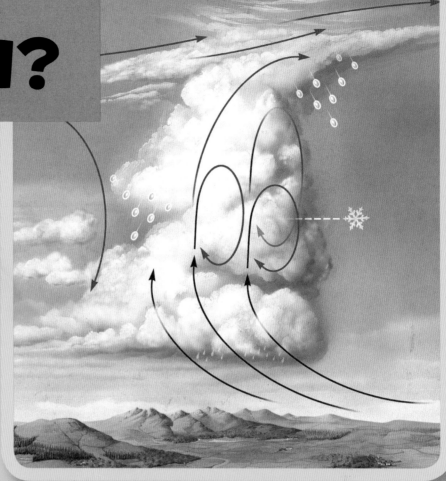

Pieces of hail are called hailstones. If you cut a hailstone in half, you will see rings. You can count the **rings** to find out how many times the hailstone went back up to the freezing-cold top of the storm before it finally fell.

86

HOW DO TORNADOES FORM?

Tornadoes can form during thunderstorms when a mass of warm, moist air meets a mass of cooler, dry air. If those masses begin swirling around each other, watch out. Strong tornadoes produce winds that spin at up to 300 miles an hour (483 km/h). They can destroy buildings, uproot trees, and throw around heavy cars and trucks as if they were toys.

The **UNITED STATES** has about **1,000** tornadoes each year. That is **MORE THAN** any other country.

Weather forecasters are getting better and better at tornado prediction—knowing when a tornado is coming. Many cities have some type of warning siren that lets people know that a tornado is nearby, so they should take shelter. If you live where there is no warning siren, stay safe by listening for radio and TV reports.

87

HOW DO EARTHQUAKES HAPPEN?

When an **EARTHQUAKE** happens under **THE OCEAN,** it can create large, damaging ocean waves called **TSUNAMIS.**

? Have **YOU EVER FELT** an earthquake?

Gigantic sheets of rock called tectonic plates move under Earth's surface. The places where their edges meet or move apart are called faults. When plates grind against each other as they move, they can get stuck, and pressure builds there. When pressure is released, the area around the fault shakes. When the plates move apart, shifting rock causes the area to shake, too. This shaking movement is an earthquake.

Tectonic plates move—and cause earthquakes—in three different ways along a fault.

Extensional: Plates move away from one another.

Compressional: Plates ram together.

Transform: Plates slide in different directions.

A **seismograph** is an instrument that measures the energy waves pulsing out from a quake's epicenter (where the quake began) and how long the movement lasts.

HOW ARE MOUNTAINS FORMED?

Tectonic plates (see page 88) sometimes push against one another. Where they meet, the land jams together and has nowhere to go but up. That creates fold mountains, which take shape over millions of years.

Block mountains are created when huge chunks of rock are pushed up.

Mountains can be formed by magma, too. Magma is melted or partly melted rock deep under Earth's surface. Gas bubbles may form inside it. As the mixture gets hotter, it expands, or grows bigger, taking up more space. Surrounded by hard rock, the hot, gassy magma pushes up through softer layers above.

Earth's highest mountain, **MOUNT EVEREST,** rises on the **BORDER OF CHINA AND NEPAL.** Mount Everest's top peak is **29,035 FEET** (8,850 m) above sea level.

A **PLATEAU** is a **FLAT AREA HIGHER** than the land around it. Over millions of years, **EROSION CAN WASH AWAY** the edges of a plateau. **HARD, ROCKY** areas are left behind.

Sometimes, magma pushes so hard that it cracks through the surface and spills or shoots out. This is a volcano. When magma reaches Earth's surface, it is called lava. Lava cools and hardens into rock. Layers of cooled lava build up over time.

Mountains can also be formed when rainwater and rivers slowly wash away dirt and softer materials. This process is called erosion.

BUILD A MOUNTAIN INVESTIGATION

You'll need whipped cream, a plate, a pan of water, and two whole (rectangular) graham crackers.

Spread the whipped cream on the plate about half an inch thick.

Dip one long edge of each graham cracker into the pan of water about an inch for one or two seconds, so each is wet along one edge. Lay the graham crackers flat on top of the whipped cream, wet halves together. Pretend these are the Earth's crust. Now gently push the two graham crackers together. See how the line where they meet (the wet edges) rises? You've just created a fold mountain.

HOW DO RIVERS FORM?

Rainwater or melting snow trickles down mountains and hills. Those trickles join other trickles, forming tiny streams. Streams flow into larger tributaries. Tributaries flow into rivers. Rivers grow larger as more and more tributaries flow into them.

Other rivers begin as springs—water flowing up from underground. The water runs downhill, joining other streams and tributaries until a river forms.

A trickle of water can cut through dirt and sand. Over time, rushing water can even carve gullies into rock. Imagine what a powerful river can do!

Rivers do not **ALWAYS** begin in mountains. Like the Mississippi River, they **MIGHT START OUT** as a narrow stream flowing from a **LAKE.**

HOW DO ROCKS FORM?

There are more than 3,000 different minerals in the world, including copper, gold, diamond, turquoise, topaz, and quartz.

Rocks are combinations of any of these minerals formed into hard chunks. There are three major types of rocks. Each one is formed in a different way.

Igneous rocks form when melted rock, or magma, cools and hardens.

Sedimentary rocks form when dirt and other materials settle, layer upon layer.

Metamorphic rocks form when heat and pressure changes one kind of rock into a new one.

? Do YOU COLLECT rocks?

93

HOW DO THE TIDES CHANGE?

Each day, ocean water rises and falls along the world's coastlines. What causes this rising and falling, called tides? Mostly, tides are caused by the position of the moon.

The moon's gravity pulls on whichever part of Earth is facing it. That pulls ocean waters toward it, making them bulge, or get bigger, for a short time. Along coastlines, the tide comes in higher, rising to cover more of the beach. As Earth slowly rotates, or turns, the tide begins falling again, covering less of the beach.

Now another part of Earth faces the moon. Tides along those coastlines rise higher and higher, and then fall again as the Earth turns.

These changing tides—rising and falling—happen once or twice each day, all around the Earth.

The **HIGHEST TIDES** in the world happen in **EASTERN CANADA'S BAY OF FUNDY.** Most tides rise **3 TO 10 FEET** (1 to 3 m). In the Bay of Fundy, tides **RISE TO 53 FEET** (16.3 m)!

HOW DO SEASONS KEEP CHANGING?

Earth slowly rotates, or turns. One full rotation takes a full day and night: 24 hours. Daytime occurs where part of Earth faces the sun. Nighttime occurs where part of Earth faces away from the sun.

But as Earth rotates, it is also slowly orbiting, or circling around, the sun. A complete orbit, one circle around the sun, takes 365 days—one year.

Now imagine Earth with a big stick through it from the North Pole to the South Pole. See how our planet is slightly tilted?

It's that small tilt that causes the changing seasons. As Earth orbits the sun, its axis (the top of that imaginary stick) always points in the same direction. So throughout the year, different parts of Earth take their turn at enjoying the sun's warmest rays.

The **EQUATOR** is an **IMAGINARY LINE** that circles the Earth. When it's **WINTER** above the Equator, it's **SUMMER** below. When it's **SUMMER** above the Equator, it's **WINTER** below.

HOW CAN SOME TREES GROW SO TALL?

A tree grows taller as it reaches for sunlight. But a tree also needs water to grow. A tree sucks water from the soil and pulls it up through its roots and trunk to its thirsty top branches and leaves.

The taller a tree grows, the harder it is to pull water to its top. That's because as the tree is trying to pull the water up, the invisible force called gravity is pulling the water down toward the ground. When a tree no longer has the strength to pull water up to its topmost leaves, it stops growing.

THE GREAT OUTDOORS

CALIFORNIA REDWOOD FACTS

Another name for the California redwood is the **SEQUOIA.**

Redwoods grow naturally along part of America's **PACIFIC COAST**— and nowhere else on Earth.

The oldest redwoods are believed to be more than **2,000 YEARS** old.

All giant redwoods begin as tiny **SEEDS** released from another redwood tree's cones.

The **TALLEST TREE** now standing is a **CALIFORNIA REDWOOD** that is 379 feet (116 m) tall. If it fell on a football field, it would reach from **ONE END ZONE PAST THE OTHER.**

How tall a tree grows also depends on what kind of tree it is. For instance, oak trees might grow to be 100 feet (31 m) tall. Most willow trees, on the other hand, rarely grow taller than about 40 feet (12 m).

California redwoods are the tallest trees in the world. That's partly because they grow in a place where temperatures don't get too hot or too cold, and where there is good soil and lots of rain.

99

Have **YOU** ever **JUMPED INTO** a pile of leaves?

HOW DO LEAVES CHANGE COLOR?

Inside every tree leaf are tiny pockets of pigment, or color, too small for human eyes to see. Those pigment pockets hold green, yellow, orange, and red.

All summer, the green pigment pockets soak up sunlight. That gives the leaves energy. They use that energy to turn water from their roots and carbon dioxide—an invisible gas in the air—into sugar. Sugar is what feeds the tree. The strong green pigments work so hard all summer that their green color covers up all the others. You see green leaves.

When fall arrives, the days grow shorter and there is less sunlight. The air gets colder. Now the tree prepares for winter by shutting off the water supply to its leaves. Without water, the green pigment cannot work. When that green pigment shuts down, other colors show through. Now you see colorful fall leaves.

As winter nears, a tree **CLOSES OFF** the small places where **LEAVES CONNECT** to its branches. Leaves fall to the ground, where they eventually **CRUMBLE** and **BECOME FOOD** for the soil.

HOW DO CLOUDS FORM?

Water droplets and ice crystals, so tiny and light that they float, hang high in the air. When billions of them bunch together, they make clouds.

But where do all these water droplets and ice crystals come from? Down here on Earth! Here's how it works: Warm air rises up from the ground. As it gets higher, the air cools. As it cools, it turns into the tiny drops of water and ice.

FACTS

Cumulus clouds are the big, fluffy **WHITE ONES.**

Clouds look white to us because they're **REFLECTING** sunlight.

Thick, gray clouds are likely filled with **RAIN.**

Airplanes create clouds called **CONTRAILS.**

Green clouds signal severe **THUNDERSTORMS** are on the way.

Have you seen clouds **MOVING QUICKLY** above? The wind **IS BLOWING** them. Sometimes they speed along as fast as **100 MILES** an hour (160 km/h)!

A cloud that hangs **NEAR THE GROUND** is called **FOG.**

Clouds don't fall because rising warm air currents beneath hold them up.

Weather experts study clouds to see what kind of weather is coming.

103

LET'S PLAY A GAME!

What in the world is pictured in the circles below? Follow the path from each one to the pictures on the right to find out.

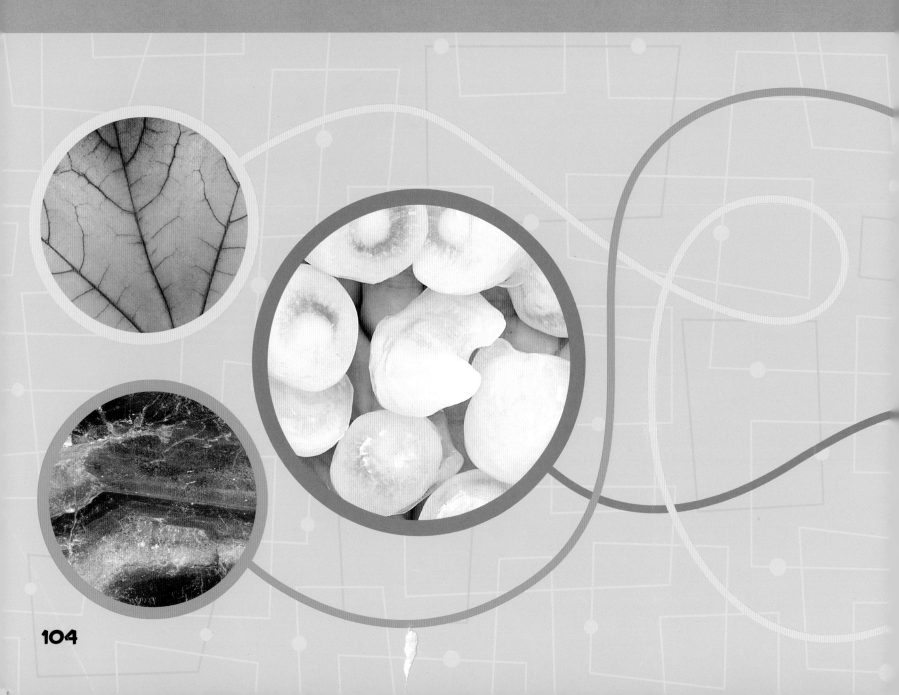

HAIL

LEAF

ROCK

How is
**ICE CREAM
MADE?**

How is
**BREAD
SLICED?**

FOOD

How are
FRUITS and
**VEGETABLES
DIFFERENT?**

HOW ARE FRUITS AND VEGETABLES DIFFERENT?

Scientists say that any food with seeds that grows on a plant is a fruit. That includes sweet foods like apples, peaches, bananas, and **cherries.** But it also includes foods people usually think of as vegetables, like corn, **cucumbers,** squash, and tomatoes.

? Which **VEGETABLE** do **YOU** like best?

Americans **EAT MORE BANANAS** than any other kind of fruit.

There are **MORE THAN 7,000** different kinds of **APPLES.**

Chefs, people whose job is to cook food, have a different way to decide if a food is a fruit or a vegetable. If a food tastes sweet and grows on a plant, it is a fruit. If a food does not taste sweet and grows on a plant, it is a vegetable.

Most **CARROTS** are orange. But they can also be **PURPLE, RED, WHITE,** or **YELLOW!**

HOW DOES FOOD GET TO THE GROCERY STORE?

Farm or orchard workers and machines pick fruits and vegetables. After they are packaged, workers load the fruits and vegetables onto trucks. The trucks deliver these fresh foods—like strawberries, apples, carrots, and spinach—to grocery stores.

Some foods are grown to be made into other foods, or processed. Wheat and other grains are made into bread products, cereals, pasta, or snacks.

Potatoes and corn might end up in a bag of chips. Many fruits and vegetables are put into cans, frozen, or made into juice. Meat might be made into hot dogs or lunch meats. Milk may be made into cheese or ice cream. Those processed foods are delivered to stores by truck, too.

Fresh and processed foods eventually arrive in a grocery store's stock room. From there, workers put them on shelves for us to buy.

? There are more than **37,000** supermarkets in the United States.

111

HOW DOES FOOD SPOIL?

Nearly all food eventually spoils, or goes bad. A banana turns spotted and brown. Carrots get rubbery. Apples get mushy. That's just the food growing old.

Sometimes food goes bad because of tiny living germs called bacteria. Bacteria are too small to see without a microscope, but they are everywhere—around us, in us, and on our food. They do not usually hurt us. Some are even good. But bacteria on food gradually take over until the food spoils.

Other foods might grow mold. That's the fuzzy green stuff growing on old bread or cheese or meat.

Foods will not spoil as fast if they are stored correctly. Molds and bacteria grow best in warm, damp places. They need air, too. That's why we keep some foods in the refrigerator or freezer. Others stay fresh kept in tightly closed containers.

MOLD INVESTIGATION

DO NOT EAT!

Take two slices of bread. Put them in separate sandwich bags and zip the bags closed tightly. Write DO NOT EAT! on the bags so nobody will eat the bread. Now, place one in the dark, cold refrigerator. Leave the other in a sunny, warm spot. Check the slices each day. How long does it take to see mold growing on one of the slices? What does that tell you about where mold grows best?

HOW IS BREAD SLICED?

If your parents bake bread at home, they use a knife to cut a loaf into slices. But bakeries use a **bread slicing machine.** In small bakeries, cooled loaves of fresh bread might be fed into a slicer one by one.

In big bakeries, freshly baked loaves ride on a moving belt through a machine that can slice as many as 65 loaves each minute. Then the belt carries the loaves to an automatic bagger.

Bakers in **PORTUGAL** baked the world's **LONGEST LOAF OF BREAD.** The loaf was more **1,325 YARDS** (1,212 m) **LONG.** That's longer than a line of 100 school buses!

HOW IS ICE CREAM MADE?

In ice cream factories, workers pour milk or cream and sugar into a large tank. They add ingredients like eggs, cocoa powder (chocolate), bits of fruit or nuts, and even globs of cookie dough. This sweet, soupy mixture is then heated in a process called pasteurizing to kill any harmful bacteria.

Ice cream is a yummy combination of this sweet mixture with tiny air bubbles and icy crystals. The next step, homogenization, keeps those three things from separating.

The final step? Enjoying spoonfuls of cold, creamy deliciousness!

VANILLA is the MOST POPULAR ice-cream FLAVOR in the United States.

? Which **ICE-CREAM FLAVOR** is your **FAVORITE?**

Cacao **BEANS** grow inside cacao **TREE PODS.** These trees grow in **HOT, RAINY** countries.

HOW IS CHOCOLATE MADE?

Making chocolate begins with cacao beans. First, the beans are roasted. Then their shells are cracked open and blown away. The broken bits of cacao left behind are called **nibs.** You could eat these nibs. But they would not taste sweet ... not yet.

FACTS

It takes about **400 BEANS** to make one pound (0.5 kg) of chocolate.

The biggest chocolate bar ever created weighed as much as an **ADULT ELEPHANT**: 12,770 pounds (5,792 kg).

Chocolate can make cats and dogs very **SICK.**

Smelling chocolate **RELAXES** your brain.

The people of **SWITZERLAND** eat more chocolate than anybody else.

The nibs are ground into a paste. Sugar, cocoa butter, vanilla, and milk are added to the paste. The mixture is ground and mashed and swirled again and again. Then it is heated and cooled many times before it is ready to become a chocolate bar.

It takes about **TEN** pounds (4.5 kg) of **MILK** to make one pound (0.5 kg) of **CHEESE.**

HOW IS CHEESE MADE?

First, cheesemakers heat milk to kill any bad bacteria. Then they put in a special, helpful bacteria. This bacteria thickens the milk and gives it flavor.

Next, an ingredient called rennet is added. Rennet separates the thickened milk into rubbery curds, or chunks, and runny whey, which is a watery liquid.

The mixture is cooked and stirred. The whey is drained off, and the curds are pressed into their final shape in wood or steel molds.

Cheesemakers add salt to preserve the cheese. Then they store the cheese in cool rooms. As the cheese ages, it reaches its final flavor.

stirring the cheese

chunks of cheese to put in molds

soaking cheese in a salt bath

cheese being shaped

HOW ARE SALT, SUGAR, AND PEPPER MADE?

SALT
Salt is collected in three ways.

1. Solar evaporation. Seawater is put into shallow ponds. Wind and sun evaporate, or dry up, the water. What is left behind? Salt.

2. Rock salt mining. Machines travel through large underground tunnels and find salt in veins—cracks or stripes in the rock. Salt is blasted out, then lifted from the mine.

3. Vacuum evaporation. Machines pump water below ground into places known to have large areas of salt. The salty water is brought aboveground and put into large tanks. The water is boiled away, leaving salt behind.

SUGAR

Most sugar comes from a tall plant called **sugarcane.** The cane is cut into small pieces, crushed, and then sprayed with hot water. This makes a mushy juice. The juice is boiled until it turns syrupy. A machine then spins the syrup, separating it into sugar crystals called raw sugar and a dark syrup called molasses. The raw sugar is shipped around the world. It is used as brown sugar or cleaned and made into pure white sugar.

Sugar can also be made from a plant called the sugar beet. Sugar beets are washed and sliced into pieces. Hot water is added to make a brown juice. The juice is boiled until it is thick and syrupy. A spinning machine separates pure white sugar from the syrup.

PEPPER

Pepper plants are flowering vines that grow up the trunks of trees in Southeast Asia. The pepper plant's berries are called **peppercorns.** Peppercorns are picked and dried, then ground up to make pepper.

LET'S PLAY A GAME!

How many things can you find that are wrong in this picture of food in silly places?

PARENT TIPS

Extend your child's experience beyond the pages of this book. Trips to libraries, museums, restaurants, zoos, or even hardware stores provide valuable educational opportunities for a child curious to know how things work. Here are some other activities you can do with National Geographic's *Little Kids First Big Book of How*.

WHAT'S THAT SMELL?
(INVESTIGATION)

Our noses can recognize thousands of smells. Have your child wait in his room while you collect strong-smelling objects from around your home. Try things like coffee, vanilla, pickle juice, peanut butter, an eraser, perfume, soap, and shampoo. Have your child close his eyes, or loosely tie a bandanna over his eyes as a blindfold. Then hold each item near his nose. Can he guess what he's smelling? Write down his answer to each smell. Have him open his eyes, or remove the blindfold. Discuss how many times he guessed correctly or incorrectly.

SPOT THE SPACE STATION
(OBSERVATION)

Have you ever spotted the International Space Station high in the night sky? Lie on a blanket in your yard and help your child find it as it passes above your area. Look here for a schedule: *spotthestation.nasa.gov*

RACING COLORS
(IMAGINATION)

Race cars are painted with numbers and bright colors, so fans can find them quickly during a race. Have your child draw a race car and then color it with bright colors and crazy patterns so hers will be the easiest to follow around the track.

DOORBELL FUN
(MEMORY)

Push your home's doorbell in a rhythmic pattern. Have your child copy the pattern. Start very simply and gradually increase difficulty.

BALANCE BUILDER
(EXERCISE)

See how long your child can stand on one foot without losing his balance. If it's too hard for him to do, ease him into it by letting him rest one foot on a box first, then removing the box carefully. Have him try it with his eyes closed.

TALL OR SMALL?
(MEASURING)

Mark the height of family members on the edge of a door. Then show your child how to use a cloth or metal tape measure to determine her height. Discuss whose height is likely to change, and whose is not.

WHALE SONGS
(IMAGINATION)

Male whales sing beautiful songs, but exactly why they do so has yet to be determined. Have your child listen to whale songs on the Internet (search "whale song audio"), and then ask him how he might sing if he were a whale. What would his hungry song be? His let's-play song? His I-need-a-hug song?

RATTLE, RATTLE
(CRAFT/DEXTERITY)

Rattlesnakes can vibrate their tails up to 90 times a second. Help your child staple two paper plates together with a handful of unpopped popcorn inside. Then have her shake it as fast as possible, like a rattlesnake shakes its tail.

RATTLESNAKE RUMBA
(IMAGINATION/EXERCISE)

Ask your child to make up a dance, using the rattle made above like a tambourine.

CARNATION TREES
(OBSERVATION)

Trees pull water from their roots up to their highest branches. To help your child understand this concept, buy a few white carnations. At home, cut half an inch from the bottom of each stem. Stand each carnation in a glass to which your child has added 20 to 30 drops of red, green yellow, or blue food coloring (or a combination). How long does it take for the carnations to pull color up into their petals?

BUILD A DINO
(CRAFT)

Paleontologists can tell by a bone's shape where it fits in a dinosaur's skeleton. Have your child draw a colorful dinosaur on the blank side of cereal box cardboard. Cut it into large pieces to create a puzzle for your child to fit back together.

MAKE ICE CREAM
(RECIPE)

Help your child make ice cream at home. You'll need: 1/2 cup milk (whole or 2 percent), 1/4 cup sugar, 1 teaspoon vanilla, ice, salt (rock salt is best), a 2-quart freezer bag, a gallon-size freezer bag, and gloves. Pour the milk, sugar, and vanilla into the smaller freezer bag. Seal tightly and set aside. Half fill the larger freezer bag with crushed ice. Add rock salt. Place the 2-quart bag inside the gallon-size bag. Seal the gallon bag tightly. Put on the gloves, and shake the bags for 10 to 15 minutes. The more you shake, the faster you will get hard ice cream.

CHOCOLATE TESTING
(OBSERVATION)

If your child can eat chocolate, help him taste a variety of flavors to introduce him to the differences. Take a nibble of dark chocolate, and then milk chocolate. Try a tiny taste of baking chocolate, followed by white chocolate.

GLOSSARY

BACTERIA: tiny living germs, some helpful, some harmful

BALLAST TANK: large metal pocket inside a submarine that holds air or water

BREACH: when a whale leaps above the ocean's surface

FAULT: a crack in Earth's surface between two giant sheets of rock

FOSSIL: the preserved remains of ancient animals or plants

FRACTURE: a broken bone

MAGMA: melted or partly melted rock deep below Earth's surface

PARALYZES: causes a body to be unable to move

POD: a group of whales

ROADBED: the flat part of the road that cars drive on

SPRING: water flowing up from underground

TSUNAMI: damaging ocean waves caused by an underwater earthquake

VIRUS: a germ that causes colds and other illnesses

ADDITIONAL RESOURCES

BOOKS

Daniels, P., C. Wilsdon, and J. Agresta. *Ultimate Bodypedia: An Amazing Inside-Out Tour of the Human Body.* Washington, DC: National Geographic Children's Books, 2014.

Goin, Miriam. *Storms!* Washington, DC: National Geographic Children's Books, 2009.

Hughes, Catherine D. *Little Kids First Big Book of Dinosaurs.* Washington, DC: National Geographic Children's Books, 2011.

Stewart, Melissa. *No Monkeys, No Chocolate.* Watertown, MA: Charlesbridge, 2013.

Tomacek, Steve. *Everything Rocks and Minerals.* Washington, DC: National Geographic Children's Books, 2011.

WEBSITES

kids.nationalgeographic.com/animals

kidshealth.org/kid/htbw

nmfs.noaa.gov/pr/pdfs/education/kids_times_whale_humpback.pdf

pbs.org/spacestation/station/issfactsheet.htm

INDEX

Boldface indicates illustrations.

FOR GREGORY –JE

National Geographic would like to thank the following panel of experts for giving their time and expertise to help us create this book:
Shannon Donahue, *Great Bear Foundation*
Christopher J. Raxworthy, Ph.D., *American Museum of Natural History*
Laura Richardson, *Teacher (first grade), Baker School, Chestnut Hill, Massachusetts*
John Umhoefer, *Wisconsin Cheese Makers Association*

Staff for This Book
Catherine Hughes, *Executive Editor, Preschool Content;* Amanda Larsen, *Art Director;* Jacqueline Kelly, *Designer;* Lori Epstein, *Senior Photo Editor;* Annette Kiesow, *Photo Editor;* Sharon K. Thompson, *Researcher;* Paige Towler, *Editorial Assistant;* Sanjida Rashid and Rachel Kenny, *Design Production Assistants;* Tammi Colleary-Loach, *Rights Clearance Manager;* Mari Robinson and Michael Cassady, *Rights Clearance Specialists;* Grace Hill, *Managing Editor;* Joan Gossett, *Senior Production Editor;* Lewis R. Bassford, *Production Manager;* George Bounelis, *Manager, Production Services;* Susan Borke, *Legal and Business Affairs*

The National Geographic Society is one of the world's largest nonprofit scientific and educational organizations. Founded in 1888 to "increase and diffuse geographic knowledge," the Society's mission is to inspire people to care about the planet. It reaches more than 400 million people worldwide each month through its official journal, *National Geographic*, and other magazines; National Geographic Channel; television documentaries; music; radio; films; books; DVDs; maps; exhibitions; live events; school publishing programs; interactive media; and merchandise. National Geographic has funded more than 10,000 scientific research, conservation, and exploration projects and supports an education program promoting geographic literacy.

For more information, please visit nationalgeographic.com, call 1-800-NGS LINE (647-5463), or write to the following address:
National Geographic Society
1145 17th Street N.W.
Washington, D.C. 20036-4688 U.S.A.

Visit us online at nationalgeographic.com/books

For librarians and teachers: ngchildrensbooks.org

More for kids from National Geographic: kids.nationalgeographic.com

For information about special discounts for bulk purchases, please contact National Geographic Books Special Sales: ngspecsales@ngs.org

For rights or permissions inquiries, please contact National Geographic Books Subsidiary Rights: ngbookrights@ngs.org

Library of Congress Cataloging-in-Publication Data

Esbaum, Jill, author.
First big book of how / by Jill Esbaum.
pages cm. -- (National geographic little kids)
Audience: Ages 4-8.
ISBN 978-1-4263-2329-4 (hardcover : alk. paper) -- ISBN 978-1-4263-2330-0 (library binding : alk. paper)
1. Technology--Miscellanea--Juvenile literature. 2. Science--Miscellanea--Juvenile literature. 3. Children›s questions and answers. I. National Geographic Society (U.S.) II. Title. III. Series: National geographic little kids.
T48.E83 2016
600--dc23
2015018148

Printed in Hong Kong
15/THK/1

Photo Credits

GI: Getty Images; IS: iStockphoto; NGC: National Geographic Creative; SS: Shutterstock
Cover (vacuum), Gunnar Pippel/SS; (train), digitalSTOCK; (chameleon), shiffti/IS; (ice cream), M. Unal Ozmen/SS; (bicycle), Ivana Jeskova/VisualCommunications/IS; (refrigerator), ppart/SS; (leaves), Peterfactors/IS; (watermelon), Zurijeta/SS; back cover (bear), Eric Isselee/SS; spine, trialhuni/SS; 2 (UP), Kuttelvaserova Stuchelova/SS; 2 (LO LE), Sanit Fuangnakhon/SS; 2 (LO RT), paul prescott/SS; 3 (LO LE), Marco Govel/SS; 3 (CTR RT), Sergey Novikov/SS; 3 (UP LE), pukach/SS; 3 (LO RT), Ilizia/SS; 4-5, Sergey Novikov/SS; 6 (UP RT), Hurst Photo/SS; 6 (LO RT), MaxyM/SS; 6 (LO LE), Ljupco Smokovski/SS; 6 (UP LE), L.M.V/SS; 7 (LO RT), Elnur/SS; 7 (UP RT), TAGSTOCK1/SS; 8, ensiferum/IS; 9 (LO), Alena Brozova/SS; 9 (UP), Sever180/SS; 9 (CTR RT), burwellphotography/IS; 10 (RT), gyn9037/SS; 10 (LE), davidp/IS; 11 (UP), Viktorus/SS; 11 (LO LE), ULKASTUDIO/SS; 11 (LO RT), MaxyM/SS; 12 (RT), Val Thoermer/SS; 12 (LE), STILLFX/SS; 13 (UP), 4Max/SS; 13 (UP RT), Fedor Selivanov/SS; 13 (CTR LE), Le Do/SS; 13 (LO), Torsak Thammachote/SS; 14 (LE), Gustoimages/Science Source; 14 (RT), Be Good/SS; 15 (LO RT), trialhuni/SS; 15 (UP), Mat Hayward/SS; 16 (RT), Anton Kozlovsky/SS; 17 (LO RT), Viorel Sima/SS; 17 (LE), Siobhan Connally/Flickr RF/GI; 18, Alex Segre/Alamy; 19 (LO), Designua/SS; 19 (UP RT), L.M.V/SS; 20 (RT), Stokkete/SS; 20 (LO CTR), Chadakorn Phalanon/SS; 21 (LO LE), aopsan/SS; 21 (RT), Tim Pannell/Corbis; 22 (LE), DenisNata/SS; 22 (LO RT), serato/SS; 23 (LO), VitalyEdush/IS; 23 (UP), Basnik/IS; 24 (LO), cpaulfell/SS; 25 (LO RT), VIP Design Inc/SS; 25 (LE), Mahathir Mohd Yasin/SS; 26-27 (both), Pixsooz/SS; 28 (LE), Monkey Business Images/SS; 28 (UP), Action Sports Photography/SS; 28 (LO), redswept/SS; 29 (LE), Dwight Nadig/IS; 29 (LO), Supertrooper/SS; 29 (UP), Andrey Armyagov/SS; 30, Monkey Business Images/SS; 31 (LO), allanw/SS; 31 (UP), donatas1205/SS; 32 (LO LE), Daniel Huerlimann-BEELDE/SS; 32 (UP RT), Alaettin Yildirim/SS; 33 (CTR RT), NuEngine/SS; 33 (cars), Rawpixel/SS; 33 (LO CTR RT), Tharakorn Arunothai/SS; 34 (UP LE), Smileus/SS; 34 (LO), sima/SS; 35 (UP), Dmitry Kalinovsky/SS; 35 (LO), IHervas/IS; 36 (LE), tome213/SS; 36-37, ventdusud/IS; 37 (LO), Orhan Cam/SS; 38-39, Pavel L Photo and Video/SS; 39 (UP), espion/IS; 40, Mandy Godbehear/SS; 41 (INSET), Vladimir Melnik/SS; 41 (UP), Susan Montgomery/SS; 41 (LO), Mindscape studio/SS; 42-43, cyoginan/IS; 43 (LO), AlbertPego/IS; 43 (UP), Serjio74/SS; 44 (LO), Anton Balazh/SS; 44 (UP), U.S. Navy/Mass Communication Specialist 1st Class Rex Nelson; 45 (LO LE), oksana2010/SS; 45 (LO RT), Buzz Pictures/Alamy; 46 (LO LE), MarcelClemens/SS; 46 (RT), Patrick H. Corkery/USAF/NASA; 47 (LO), NASA/ISS; 47 (UP), lexaarts/SS; 47 (CTR RT), NASA/ISS; 48 (LO LE), ventdusud/IS; 48 (CTR), donatas1205/SS; 48 (UP RT), loraks/SS; 48 (LO RT), zhangyang13576997233/SS; 49 (UP RT), U.S. Navy/Mass Communication Specialist 1st Class Rex Nelso; 49 (UP LE), Mindscape studio/SS; 49 (LO LE), Patrick H. Corkery/USAF/NASA; 49 (CTR), AlbertPego/IS; 49 (LO RT), Pavel L Photo and Video/SS; 50 (UP LE), picturepartners/SS; 50 (UP RT), Jaimie Duplass/SS; 50 (LO), Zurijeta/SS; 51 (UP LE), szefei/IS; 51 (UP RT), Peter Gudella/SS; 51 (LO LE), JGI/Jamie Grill/Blend Images/Corbis; 51 (LO RT), GoneWithTheWind/SS; 52 (RT), Lightspring/SS; 52 (LO LE), Serhiy Kobyakov/SS; 53 (UP), AuntSpray/SS; 53 (LO), Hung Chung Chih/SS; 54 (LE), wang song/SS; 54 (UP), Kameel4u/SS; 55 (LO), Ilya Andriyanov/SS; 55 (UP), KidStock/Blend Images/Corbis; 56, 2/Jonathan Kirn/Ocean/Corbis; 57 (UP), Hurst Photo/SS; 57 (LO), connel/SS; 58 (LO), Gunita Reine/SS; 58 (CTR), Kalmatsuy/SS; 59 (UP), Peter Kotoff/SS; 59 (LO), Victoria Shapiro/SS; 60 (LE), Dorling Kindersley RF/GI; 60 (RT), Gelpi JM/SS; 61 (LE), princessdlaf/IS; 61 (RT), borisovv/SS; 62 (LO), spfotocz/SS; 62 (UP), Inmagine/Alamy; 63 (UP RT), Volodymyr Krasyuk/SS; 63 (LO LE), Kalin Eftimov/SS; 63 (CTR), 4774344sean/IS; 64 (CTR), Shubhangi G. Kene/Alamy; 64 (RT), bikeriderlondon/SS; 65 (LO), Carlos Caetano/SS; 65 (UP), Elena Schweitzer/SS; 66 (2), Gelpi JM/SS; 66 (5), Samuel Borges Photography/SS; 66 (6), hawridger/IS; 66 (1), Samuel Borges Photography/SS; 66 (3), Rob Marmion/SS; 66 (7), Monkey Business Images/SS; 66 (4), Samuel Borges Photography/SS; 67 (12), Andresr/SS; 67 (6), princessdlaf/IS; 67 (1), Samuel Borges Photography/SS; 67 (7), Samuel Borges Photography/SS; 67 (9), Samuel Borges Photography/SS; 67 (4), Gelpi JM/SS; 67 (8), Gelpi JM/SS; 67 (3), Samuel Borges Photography/SS; 67 (10), Gelpi JM/SS; 67 (2), rimglow/IS; 67 (11), Gelpi JM/SS; 67 (5), rimglow/IS; 68 (UP LE), WaterFrame/Alamy; 68 (UP RT), David Aleksandrowicz/SS; 68 (LO), Adam Van Spronsen/SS; 69 (UP), alexskopje/SS; 69 (LO), xlt974/SS; 70, larus/SS; 71 (UP), Joel Sartore/NGC; 71 (LO), Robert Eastman/SS; 72, Richard A McMillin/SS; 73 (UP LE), Jeff Rotman/NaturePL; 73 (UP RT), Rich Carey/SS; 73 (LO), Paul Nicklen/NGC; 74 (LE), Ronald Wittek/Photographer's Choice RF/GI; 74 (RT), Sven-Erik Arndt/Picture Press RM/GI; 75 (UP), frikota/SS; 75 (INSET), siridhata/SS; 75 (LO), Dieter Meyrl/IS; 76 (UP), Eric Isselee/SS; 76 (LO), Heiko Kiera/SS; 77, eAlisa/SS; 78, melissaf84/SS; 79 (UP), Paul S. Wolf/SS; 79 (LO [all]), Joy Brown/SS; 79 (LO [all]), Joy Brown/SS; 79 (LO [all]), Joy Brown/SS; 80 (CTR), Maria Stenzel/NGC; 80 (LO), Francoise de Valera/Alamy; 81, Marques/SS; 82 (bear), Rosa Jay/SS; 82 (octopus), WaterFrame/Alamy; 82 (camel), Iakov Filimonov/SS; 82 (chameleon), Fedor Selivanov/SS; 82 (rattlesnake), Tom Reichner/SS; 82 (jellyfish), Ritu Manoj Jethani/SS; 83 (beaver), Jody Ann/SS; 83 (whale), Paul S. Wolf/SS; 83 (camel), Iakov Filimonov/SS; 83 (bear), Rosa Jay/SS; 83 (octopus), WaterFrame/Alamy; 83 (rattlesnake), Tom Reichner/SS; 83 (jellyfish), Ritu Manoj Jethani/SS; 83 (chameleon), Fedor Selivanov/SS; 84 (UP LE), trubavin/SS; 84 (LO LE), Olga Popova/SS; 84-85 (LO), Ammit Jack/SS; 85 (UP LE), Carsten Peter/NGC; 85 (UP CTR), Tyler Boyes/SS; 85 (UP RT), kisa kuyruk/SS; 85 (LO RT), Kichigin/SS; 86 (UP RT), Gary Hincks/Science Source; 86 (LO LE), Suzanne Tucker/SS; 86 (LO RT), Science Source; 87 (UP), R. Gino Santa Maria/SS; 87 (LO), Mike Theiss/NGC; 88 (LE), NigelSpiers/SS; 88 (RT), JIJI PRESS/AFP/GI; 89 (LE), Henning Dalhoff/Science Source; 89 (RT), Cico/SS; 90 (UP), Yongyut Kumsri/SS; 90 (LO), Curioso/SS; 91 (1), Viktor1/SS; 91 (2), Ilya Akinshin/SS; 91 (3), M. Unal Ozmen/SS; 91 (4), Coprid/SS; 91 (5), Louella938/SS; 92 (UP), Florin Stana/SS; 92 (LO), Jason Lindsey/Alamy; 93 (UP), vvoe/SS; 93 (CTR), elenaburn/SS; 93 (LO CTR), maxim ibragimov/SS; 93 (LO LE), Francesco R. Iacomino/SS; 94-95, James Crotty/Alamy; 95 (CTR LE), V. J. Matthew/SS; 95 (RT), Josef Hanus/SS; 96 (LO), Sailorr/SS; 96 (UP RT), jimmyjamesbond/IS; 97 (UP), YanLev/SS; 97 (LO), Chin Kit Sen/SS; 98, emresenkartal/SS; 99, Jamie Pham/Alamy; 100, maxslu/SS; 101 (UP), rodho/SS; 101 (CTR), pukach/SS; 101 (LO LE), Madlen/SS; 101 (LO), Brand X; 102 (LO), Merkushev Vasiliy/SS; 102-103 (UP), Bplanet/SS; 103 (RT), Patrick Foto/SS; 104 (UP LE), pukach/SS; 104 (LO LE), elenaburn/SS; 104 (CTR), Suzanne Tucker/SS; 105 (CTR RT), pukach/SS; 105 (LO), elenaburn/SS; 105 (UP), Suzanne Tucker/SS; 106 (UP LE), slava17/SS; 106 (LO), Alena Ozerova/SS; 106-107 (UP), raifu/SS; 107 (UP RT), Alex Staroseltsev/SS; 107 (LO), monticello/SS; 108 (UP), Zsolt Biczo/SS; 108 (LO), Anna Sedneva/SS; 109 (UP LE), Iconotec; 109 (RT), rimglow/IS; 109 (LO), Enlightened Media/SS; 110 (LO), Julie Ann Fineman/Corbis; 110 (UP), Gwoeii/SS; 111 (UP LE), S_E/SS; 111 (RT), kurhan/SS; 112 (LE), Voyagerix/SS; 112 (LO), Artography/SS; 113 (UP), Dani Vincek/SS; 113 (CTR), snyferok/IS; 113 (LO), Canadapanda/SS; 113 (LO), Canadapanda/SS; 113 (CTR), snyferok/IS; 114 (UP), safakcakir/SS; 114 (LO), Zdenka Darula/SS; 115 (LE), Blend Images/Alamy; 115 (RT), M. Unal Ozmen/SS; 116 (UP LE), Luiscar74/SS; 116 (LO), Diana Taliun/SS; 116 (UP RT), Vilainecrevette/SS; 117 (LE), urfin/SS; 117 (UP RT), Brand X; 117 (LO), Marco Govel/SS; 118, Brent Hofacker/SS; 119 (UP LE), Sarah2/SS; 119 (UP RT), Olaf Speier/SS; 119 (LO RT), francesco de marco/SS; 119 (LO LE), racorn/SS; 120 (UP LE), Danny Smythe/SS; 120 (LO), Discovod/SS; 120 (UP CTR), Givaga/SS; 121 (UP), Izf/SS; 121 (RT), saiko3p/SS; 122 (asparagus), Lightspring/SS; 122 (girl), Nanette Grebe/SS; 122 (ice cream scoops), M. Unal Ozmen/SS; 122 (squirrel), IrinaK/SS; 122 (pizza), images.etc/SS; 122-123 (background), Serg64/SS; 122 (fence), inxti/SS; 122 (tomato), Tim UR/SS; 122 (carrot), Spauln/IS; 122 (ice cream cone), M. Unal Ozmen/SS; 123 (strawberries), bajinda/SS; 123 (dog), Eric Isselee/SS; 123 (boy), Luis Louro/SS; 123 (cheese), valzan/SS; 123 (building), S_E/SS; 123 (spaghetti), Sergey Molchenko/SS; 123 (bench), studioaraminta/IS; 123 (toast), exopixel/SS; 123 (cabbage), monticello/SS; 123 (loaf of bread), Monebook/SS